Mysterious Encounters

Fairies

by Jan Burns

KIDHAVEN PRESS

An imprint of Thomson Gale, a part of The Thomson Corporation

THOMSON

GALE

Detroit • New York • San Francisco • New Haven, Conn. • Waterville, Maine • London

© 2007 Thomson Gale, a part of The Thomson Corporation.

Thomson and Star Logo are trademarks and Gale and KidHaven Press are registered trademarks used herein under license.

For more information, contact
KidHaven Press
27500 Drake Rd.
Farmington Hills, MI 48331-3535
Or you can visit our Internet site at http://www.gale.com

LIBRARY OF CONGRESS CATALOGING-IN-PUBLICATION DATA

Burns, Jan.
  Fairies / by Jan Burns.
    p. cm. — (Mysterious encounters)
  Includes bibliographical references and index.
  ISBN-13: 978-0-7377-3635-9 (hardcover)
  1. Fairies—Juvenile literature. I. Title.
  BF1552.B87 2007
  133.1'4—dc22

                                                    2007006885

ISBN-10: 0-7377-3635-6
Printed in the United States of America

Contents

Chapter 1

The Fairy Kingdom

Most people think that fairies exist only in stories for children. Many of the people who claim to have encountered fairies also thought that at one time. Their personal experiences with fairies, however, convinced them to change their minds, and they now believe in a **supernatural** world.

The Secret Commonwealth

In 1691 Reverend Robert Kirk claimed that when he was walking near his home in Aberfoyle, Scotland, he encountered fairies. The experience changed his life. He wanted to learn everything he could about the supernatural beings, so he interviewed others who claimed that they had also seen fairies. He wrote a book called *The Secret Commonwealth* that contained what he learned from these interviews, as well as his own experiences. Kirk eventually came to believe that he had been gifted with **second sight**, sometimes called clairvoyance, which gave him the ability to see things (like fairies) that most people could not see.

"They are distributed in tribes and orders, and have children, marriages, deaths and burials in appearance even as we," wrote Kirk in *The Secret Commonwealth*. "The fairies live a life very much like our own with clothing similar to that of the people whose country in which they live."[1]

Fairy History

Fairy beliefs have existed in every traditional society for centuries. Although fairy encounters like the one above have been reported all over the world, most of

Second Sight

Second sight is a person's ability to perceive information about objects, places, and events without the use of normal senses. Researchers say it can be inherited and believe that it can also develop after a blow to the head.

The classic image of a female fairy with delicate wings.

them have occurred in England, Scotland, Ireland, and Wales. Only a little over 100 years ago the existence of fairies was widely accepted in the rural areas of these countries.

Some people believe fairies still live alongside of humans, but most people cannot see them because they exist in a kind of **fourth dimension**, a fairy realm that humans cannot freely enter. According to some stories, fairies can make themselves visible to humans whenever they want.

Legends and stories tell of more than 170 different types of fairies. They include elves, imps, dwarves, urchins, hobs, goblins, and many others. Each fairy species has its own features and characteristics, so one type of fairy can be very different from another fairy type. Some are basically good, while others are troublemakers. Although some are said to be as tall as or taller than humans, most are described as much shorter than humans. Elves tend to be slender and have pointed ears. Goblins are scary-looking, with grotesque, distorted bodies, and dwarves are usually stocky, muscular, and bearded. To further complicate things, fairies are

All fairies possess the power to enchant, which makes them potentially dangerous.

believed to be **shape-shifters**, beings that have the ability to appear to people in any form they choose.

While the various types of fairies may look quite different from each other, they share certain powers, characteristics, and habitats. All fairies possess the power to **enchant**, which makes them potentially dangerous. Also, all fairies can appear and disappear, change the appearance of other things, and fly or move from place to place instantly. They love beautiful music and dancing, like to reward the good-hearted, and bring misfortune to the greedy.

Some fairies are homebodies, or house elves. They find a family and move in with them. Then, they cook, clean, sew, and work at any other household chores that need to be done. People describe them as being very small and wrinkled-looking.

Hard or Soft Phenomena?

Hard phenomena leave behind visible traces, such as the tracks of an unknown creature or radar records of an unidentified flying object (UFO)—evidence that can be found and analyzed to yield detailed information. Soft phenomena, like fairies, leave no physical traces for scientists or others to examine, only the witnesses' accounts.

Mermaids, which resemble human females but have the lower bodies of fish, are a type of fairy.

These fairies usually dress in brown or gray rags and wear pointed red caps.

Most fairy encounters occur outdoors, particularly in flower gardens, forests, or stretches of wilderness. These fairies are called pixies or tree sprites. They are different shades of green and brown that blend in with their environment. Other fairies, such as mermaids and selkies are seen only near water. Mermaids resemble human females but have the lower bodies of fish, which typically can change from hues of blue, green, and even gold as the sunlight bounces off of them. Selkies look like seals, but they can transform to human form by shedding their seal skins. Sailing captains long ago dropped coins into the water for both mermaids and selkies when sailing past well-known watery fairy sites, to pay for the safe passage of their ships.

Although many fairy characteristics are well known, there is disagreement as to exactly what fairies are and where they came from. One theory holds that fairies might be members of prehistoric tribes who fled into the hills, underground, or wilderness to escape invading conquerors. Sightings could be encounters with the last survivors of this race. Some people believe that fairies are fallen angels or even spirits of the dead, who are somehow caught between the worlds of the living and the dead. Some say they are just stories, imagined creatures, legends that have been passed down from generation to generation. Whatever the case, some have claimed to have had real encounters with fairies.

Typical Fairy Encounters

On April 30, 1973, children's author Mary Treadgold was traveling by bus through Mull, Scotland, when something incredible happened:

"My bus drew into a lay-by (an area by the side of the road) and I looked idly at an expanse of peat outside the window. This tiny young man, about eighteen inches tall, was standing beside a clump of tallish heather with his foot on a spade."[2]

Treadgold said he had a thin face, tight, brown, curly hair, and was wearing blue jeans and a very white shirt. He made her think of a leprechaun. She was positive that he was not a child, saying he was a perfectly formed living being like any of us, proportioned like a grown person, only in miniature.

When she returned home to London she talked to a friend who came from that area of Scotland. Her friend told her that friends of hers had also seen small people on Mull, and that Mull was known to be a site where fairies lived.

This encounter is similar to many that **folklorist** and writer Janet Bord has studied. In her book *Fairies: Real Encounters with Little People,* she explains that many fairy encounters have things in common. In most cases the people who see fairies are alone, often out at night, and are in a relaxed state of mind, not thinking about anything in particular. Soon afterward they see the fairy (or fairies).

Bord reports that most encounters usually last only a short time, and there is not much interaction between the person and the fairy. The fairy may look directly at the person, or might even smile,

Goblins are reported to be scary-looking, with grotesque, distorted bodies.

Supernatural or Paranormal?

Supernatural phenomena, like fairies, involve powers or spirits that do not belong to the natural world. By contrast, **paranormal** phenomena like clairvoyance are usually believed to be the result of some sort of natural power that is not yet known.

but then it goes about its business, ignoring the person. Most people involved in fairy encounters say the experience is so shocking and unexpected that they will remember it for the rest of their lives.

Through the years, the reports of fairy encounters have varied widely. Some of the meetings have been enchanting, and some have been scary. Some reports are of brief sightings. Some are tales of lengthy encounters and interactions that totally changed the lives of the people who had the encounter. Some are legends told generation after generation. Although no one has been able to prove fairies exist, the reports of fairy encounters continue.

Chapter 2

Enchanting Encounters

Some fairies are known for helping deserving people in need. Devas are nature spirits who teach people about gardening. Brownies like to keep houses neat by helping with daily cleaning chores, and elves often reward people who have treated them kindly.

Healing Powers

One of the best-documented cases of a fairy encounter happened in Cornwall, England, in 1645. Nineteen-year-old Anne Jeffries had been fascinated with fairies since childhood. She wanted to see one so much that she searched for them among flowers, where she thought they might live. She even learned a rhyme that was supposed to attract fairies: "Fairy fair and fairy bright, come and be my chosen sprite."[3]

Jeffries claimed that six fairies kidnapped her while she was knitting in her garden one day. One of the fairies put his hands over her eyes, and she felt a sensation of flying through the air. After they landed she was reduced to their small size and taken to what she believed was fairyland.

She said that it was an incredibly beautiful place, with palaces of gold and silver and a garden full of exotic flowers and fruit trees. Jeffries happily joined in with the fairies when they asked her to dance. Eventually one of them put his hands over her eyes, and she once again felt herself being lifted into the

In 1645 Anne Jeffries claimed she was kidnapped by fairies.

Fairy Healers

Fairies are said to have expert knowledge of herbs that have medicinal powers, such as yarrow, vervain, eyebright, and many others. They are careful to gather and prepare them in a special manner to ensure that they will work. Besides the natural properties these herbs possess, the fairies are said to weave magic into the herbs to increase their healing power.

air. She woke up later near her home, dazed and lying on the ground.

Jeffries later claimed that as a result of that visit and others with the fairies, she developed the power to heal people's illnesses. She said the fairies taught her that certain plants and herbs possessed special medicinal qualities. In addition, she found that after her fairy encounter she was able to go for long periods of time without eating human food. She said it was because the fairies brought her fairy food.

Jeffries worked as a servant for Moses Pitt and his family. Records reveal that Pitt even wrote a letter to the bishop of Gloucester about Jeffries' extraordinary change in eating habits. He wrote, "She forsook eating our victuals, and was fed by these fairies from that time to the next Christmas-day; upon which day she came to our table and said, because it was that day, she would eat some roast beef with us, the which she did."[4]

People from all over southern England traveled to see Jeffries, and her fame as a fairy-inspired healer spread. Unfortunately, because of her new abilities she was accused of being a witch. She was sent to prison and ordered not to be given any food. Records show that she remained in prison without food for a long period and that she remained in good health. She said she survived because the fairies brought her fairy food to eat. She was eventually released from prison due to lack of evidence that she was a witch.

The Findhorn Garden

Another enchanting encounter with fairies occurred in Findhorn, Scotland. In 1962 Peter

In the 1960s, it was claimed that fairies helped the gardens at Findhorn to flourish. Pictured here are some residents of Findhorn Ecovillage in 1997.

Caddy, his wife Eileen, and their three sons moved with their friend Dorothy Maclean to this coastal village, which lies near the Arctic Circle. They decided to grow a large vegetable garden to try to support themselves. Although they had a lot of enthusiasm and determination, all the facts pointed against their having any kind of gardening success. Besides having a cold climate, Findhorn's soil was so filled with sand and rocks that trying to plant a garden there seemed foolish.

Things were not going too well with the garden when Maclean claimed that a deva contacted her and offered to help the group. The deva said she would tell them where to plant certain crops, what types of soil the different plants needed, how far apart to plant them, and how much water to give the plants. Caddy then claimed that elves also gave the group additional advice not only about gardening, but about the need for people to love one another.

Psychic Powers

It is possible that the senses of psychic people interpret, or sense, the supernatural in different ways, some visually, some aurally (through hearing), and some by inner sensations.

Findhorn Ecovillage is a place where residents strive to live in balance and harmony with the natural energies of Earth.

The group followed the fairies' directions. They were astonished to see their garden flourish with vegetables, herbs, and flowers. Many even grew to enormous sizes. The garden produced cabbages, broccoli, and other vegetables that weighed over ten times their usual weights. Within a short time the garden was supplying the group with more than enough food.

News spread about their amazing garden, and horticultural experts from around the world traveled to Findhorn to examine the soil, the growing conditions, and everything grown there. They found no simple scientific explanation for the garden's success. They said by all accounts the garden should have failed. The Findhorn garden seemed to defy all traditional rules of gardening.

Eventually the group added many more members and became known as the Findhorn Foundation. They started a college as well as an ecovillage where people strive to live in balance and harmony with the natural energies of Earth.

The Elves of Lily Hill Farm

Penny Kelly was a teacher, but she wanted to do something totally different with her life. Because of this, in 1987 she and her husband bought 57 acres (23ha) of land with a 100-year-old house, a rickety barn, and a 13-acre run-down vineyard (5ha) in Lawton, Michigan.

An elf is depicted in Richard Doyle's painting *An Evening Ride.*

Seeing Fairies

"Those people who are lucky enough to see fairies not just once but often are likewise more sensitive than most of us to emanations, or things, passing through the invisible curtain which seems to separate us from the world where the Little People live," according to Janet Bord, folklorist and author of *Fairies: Real Encounters with Little People.*

At first Kelly thought that buying the property was the right thing to do, but as time passed, she was not so sure. She knew little about gardening, and nothing at all about raising grapes. She was worried that she and her husband would lose all the money they had invested in the property if they could not adequately repair it and make the vineyard healthy again.

While walking in the vineyard one day, Kelly claimed she was approached by three elves. At first she could not believe that she was really seeing them. They convinced her, however, that they wanted to help her improve the property. They told her it had fallen into disrepair after years of neglect and after poisonous chemicals had been sprayed on the plants and soil.

They said they would work with her to improve the vineyard if she would follow their instructions and work in balance and harmony with nature. This meant she could not use any chemical fertilizers or pesticides. Instead, the elves taught her about the importance of healthy soil, disease-resistant plants, and the use of native plants and **heirloom seeds**. They said these things would make the vineyard healthy again.

Under the elves' supervision, Kelly and her husband had to do a tremendous amount of physical labor. They had to clear the land of all diseased or dead plants as well as remove the unhealthy soil. Then good soil had to be brought in and shoveled or raked into the ground to replace what they had removed, to bring the soil up to the right level. New plants were then planted according to the elves' directions.

As a result of her contact with the elves, Kelly and her husband were able to substantially improve the property and bring it back to a healthy state. She described her experience, which changed her life and her values, in her book *The Elves of Lily Hill Farm: A Partnership with Nature*. She said she learned to work in balance and harmony with nature.

The fairies in these three stories all were tremendously helpful to the people they encountered. However, some fairy encounters have been frightening and dangerous.

Chapter 3

Scary Fairies

Most fairies are mischievous but fun-loving beings who love to dance, listen to music, and enjoy life. Some fairies, however, can be dangerous and will punish anyone who disturbs their dwellings, favorite trees, or fields and paths.

Fairy Revenge

Bord has found numerous instances where fairies have supposedly taken revenge against people who have not heeded warnings about crossing them. One such case occurred in 1907 in County Londonderry, Northern Ireland. An elderly farmer named John M'Laughlin cut down a holly bush despite his neighbor's warning that the bush was a fairy favorite.

A mischievous goblin can cause harm to a household if he is disturbed.

M'Laughlin then used the bush's branches to clean and sweep out his chimney.

Strange things immediately started to happen around M'Laughlin's home. He found the soot and ashes he had removed from his chimney dumped back into his kitchen. He also found lumps of soot smeared onto his walls and thrown in among his kitchen utensils. Stones mysteriously crashed onto his roof and then fell inside the house and onto the floors without making any holes in the roof.

Witnesses claim they also observed the following happen inside M'Laughlin's house:

A piece of brick in a closed cupboard was seen to hurl itself across the kitchen and smash into seven or eight pieces against the window sash. A two-pound stone, used as a griddle balance, was also observed to dash about. After negotiating two successive corners, it passed through the closed door into the parlour, where it smashed the window and tore a hole in the curtain.[5]

No one was able to find a way to stop the vandalism, and M'Laughlin eventually was forced to abandon his home.

Angry Fairies

In his book *Encounters with the Unknown,* writer Colin Parsons states that fairies can change their helpful attitude and behavior abruptly and turn into nasty nuisances if they feel they have been mistreated. He tells about a couple, Mr. and Mrs. Bolton, who moved into a new home in England. They were astonished when the former homeowners told them that brownies lived in the garden and did chores for the family.

The couple soon observed startling things happening in their new home. While they were both away at work, dishes were washed, their laundry was cleaned in their washing machine, and the

Superstition

Some people think that superstition plays a large role in fairy encounters. Superstitions are beliefs that have no basis in fact. Often they come about through fear or ignorance. People start to believe that something is true either because of a mistaken belief or because someone they trust has told them it is true.

clothes dried in their dryer. At first Mrs. Bolton thought that perhaps she had simply done these chores herself and just forgotten that she had done them. But when these things continued, she knew someone else was doing them.

Her husband also noticed strange happenings. When he went to do chores he discovered they were already done. He found the garden shed all tidied up and his clothes gathered up to be washed or already hung up in the closet. Yet he was positive that neither he nor his wife had done any of these things themselves.

Then one day Mrs. Bolton lost her temper with the brownies about something they had done. They suddenly stopped being helpful and started making huge messes around the house. The Boltons found that "soap powder had been tipped all over the vegetables, [water] taps had been turned on and plugs

Brownies are thought of as clean, helpful fairies.

Super Powers

Statistics show that people want to believe in individuals of this world, or another, who have powers that cannot be explained. They want to believe the impossible is possible.

put in, furniture had been knocked over and jam rubbed into the Persian carpet."[6]

Things eventually got so bad that the couple had to move out of the house.

Trespassing on Fairy Grounds

Another scary encounter was reported by Reverend Doctor Edward Williams, who was a well-respected eighteenth-century minister. He wrote that in 1757, when he was seven years old, he and his sister were playing with some children in a field in northern Wales. They suddenly saw a group of beings dancing about 100 yards away from them.

"They were all clothed in red, a dress not unlike a military uniform, without hats, but their heads tied with handkerchiefs of a reddish color. They appeared of a size somewhat less than our own, but more like dwarfs than children,"[7] Williams said.

The children questioned each other about what the little people could be, since they did not look like any humans they had ever seen before. Suddenly, one of the fairies started to run after

Williams, possibly because he was the smallest of the group. Another one of the fairies shouted at him in an unknown language. Frightened, the children ran toward an open gate to escape.

Williams looked back and "saw the grim elf just at my heels, having a full and clear, though terrific view of him, with his ancient, swarthy, and grim complexion."[8] The fairy grabbed out for Williams. Luckily, just at that minute his sister pulled him through the gate to safety.

The children quickly ran home and alerted their families. The group searched the whole area, but the fairies had disappeared by then. Williams later said he was puzzled by this incident for the rest of his life, because it could not be explained in any

The Dance of the Little People, by William Holmes Sullivan.

normal way. Did he and the other children stumble onto a favorite fairy playground?

Fairy Punishment

Another possible case of fairy retaliation occurred in 1920 in Kiltimagh, Ireland. People there planned to build a new hospital. Unfortunately, two thorn trees that according to folklore were favored by fairies grew in the chosen area, and the hospital could not be built without cutting one of them down. It was extremely difficult to find someone who dared to do the job, but finally such a man was found.

Before he started work others warned him not to do it because the fairies would punish him. He just laughed and cut the tree down. Afterward he joked about the fairies harming him because of what he had done.

An illustration of a tree fairy.

Strangely enough, that night the man had a stroke. He lay in a crippled state for almost a year before he died. Some people claimed he would still be alive if he would have listened to the warnings about fairies and left the tree alone.

Road Altered

The reluctance to hurt a fairy site cropped up again in 1968, when it was reported that the course of a new road in Donegal, Ireland, had to be altered because workmen refused to cut down a tree that was said to be favored by fairies. According to contractor Roy Green, "I refused to cut it down, and I would not order any of my men to do the job. I have heard so much about these fairy trees that I would not risk it."[9]

Another contractor was asked to do the work, but he also refused. "There is something uncanny about it," he said. "The roots are not more than a couple of feet below ground—yet it defied a hurricane seven years ago."[10]

In each fairy encounter the facts of the case have to be examined to see if they are believable. Since there is rarely hard evidence to prove the encounter

Fairy Evidence?

Some intriguing objects that some people claim once belonged to fairies have been discovered. A tiny shoe was found in southwestern Ireland in 1835. The shoe, believed to be made of mouse skin, was 2 7/8 inches long and 7/8 of an inch wide. It was styled like the type of shoe that an eighteenth-century gentleman might have worn. Amazingly, it was worn down on the heel, which does not seem likely if it was a doll's shoe. A second shoe of this type was later found, also in Ireland.

It is considered bad luck by many to damage or cut down trees that are favored by fairies.

occurred, investigators are left with just the word of witnesses. The two fairy encounters in the following chapter are famous because of the great excitement they caused when they happened. Questions remain unanswered about both of them today.

Chapter 4

Famous Fairy Encounters

People are fascinated and puzzled by reports of fairy encounters. They want to know all the details of the incidents so they can decide for themselves if they are believable or not. The following two fairy encounters caused great debates between people who believed the encounters were real and those who thought they were **hoaxes**.

The Green Children of Suffolk

Villagers in Wolf-Pits (now known as Woolpits), England, in the 12th century were astonished after two small children were found crying outside the entrance to a nearby cave. The boy and girl were dressed in clothing made from a material that the

Fact or Fantasy?

villagers had never seen before, and neither child could speak English. Instead, they talked in a strange language that no one understood. Strangest of all, the children had green skin. This caused great excitement because it was widely believed in England at the time that fairies had green skin.

Although they seemed to be starving, the children refused to eat any of the food that was offered to them until someone brought them some beans. They ate these hungrily. This amazed the villagers because at the time beans were believed to be the traditional food of the dead. Because of this and the children's strange appearance, the villagers believed the children were fairies who had somehow strayed into the human world.

The boy died shortly after they were found, but the girl survived. The green color of her skin eventually faded and she learned to speak English. When she told the villagers about her background, her answers only deepened the mystery.

She said she and her brother came from a country called St. Martin's Land, a place where it was always dim twilight because there was no sun, and the people there were all green like her. She and her brother had been guarding a flock of animals when they heard the ringing of bells. Curious, they followed the sound deep down into an underground passageway until they eventually came out into the daylight. They were found by the villagers soon afterwards.

People who did not believe the story claimed that the children were probably lost human children.

A group of fairies gather around a child, forming a fairy ring.

Fairyland

Fairies are believed to live underground in deep mines or caves. Most descriptions of fairyland describe it as reached through a hole in the ground or a hill.

They thought the children's skin was green simply because they were undernourished. They were unable to explain, however, why no parents ever came forward to claim the children, although news about them was circulated throughout England. Medieval **chronicler** William of Newburgh wrote this about the green children story:

> Although the thing is asserted by many, yet I have long been in doubt about the matter, deeming it ridiculous to credit a thing supported by no rational foundation, yet, in the end, was so overwhelmed by the weight of so many competent witnesses that I have been compelled to believe and wonder over a matter I was unable to comprehend and unravel by the powers of my intellect.[11]

The Cottingley Fairy Photos

The families of ten-year-old Frances Griffiths and her thirteen-year-old cousin Elsie Wright did not believe the girls when they claimed they saw fairies in a nearby wooded area in Cottingley, England, in 1917. To prove their story, the next time they went into the woods the girls brought a camera with them and took pictures of four tiny, winged fairies. Their parents, however, did not believe the photos were real. They were convinced that the girls had simply photographed paper cutouts of fairies. The girls denied they had done anything like that.

The following year Frances wrote to a friend in South Africa. In her letter she said that she and Elsie were very friendly with the fairies in the area. She also sent copies of her fairy photos along with her letter. On the back of one of the pictures she wrote, "Elsie and I are very freindly (sic) with the beck [wood] fairies."[12]

A photo of Frances Griffiths and the Cottingley fairies, which was ultimately proven to be a hoax.

Arthur Conan Doyle firmly believed in the story of the Cottingley fairies.

In 1920 Elsie's mother, Polly Wright, attended a folklore lecture where belief in fairies was discussed. Wright mentioned that her daughter had some fairy photos. Eventually she lent the photos to Edward Gardner, a man who was deeply interested in the spiritual world.

Sir Arthur Conan Doyle, the writer who created Sherlock Holmes, heard about the photos and urged Gardner to take the pictures to a London photo lab to be analyzed. There, as Doyle later reported, "two experts were unable to find any flaw, but refused to testify to the genuineness of them, in view of some possible trap."[13]

Doyle believed the photos to be real, so he told newspaper reporters that the experts did not declare them fakes. The story was then given worldwide publicity, probably because of Doyle's comments. Once the photos were made public, most of the people who saw them thought the photos were obvious hoaxes. They wondered how Doyle could have believed they were real.

It turned out that after the recent death of his son, Doyle had developed a strong belief in the existence of a supernatural, or spiritual, world. He had desperately wanted to find proof that such a world existed. He thought the pictures provided that proof. Doyle was criticized by some people who said that he ignored the evidence altogether.

Despite this, attempts at the time to prove that the pictures were fakes were unsuccessful. Famous magician Harry Houdini claimed that the fairy figures in the photos were the same as those shown in an advertising poster that was popular at the time. He suspected that the fairies pictured on the poster

Fairy Music

People who have encountered fairies often say they heard music that seemed to come out of nowhere before seeing the fairy. One person described it as the sweetest music he had ever heard. Others have called the music so entrancing they felt they had to follow it.

Although most often the music has been heard above ground, there are also many accounts of people hearing music coming from under the ground.

could have been cut out or copied. However, he was eventually found to be wrong about this.

In the following years stories were written about the Cottingley fairy photos in newspapers and magazines. People developed strong beliefs about them. People who believed in the existence of fairies tried to convince others that the photos were real. At the same time, nonbelievers made fun of the photos.

Many years later the girls, who by that time were grown women, finally admitted that Wright had cut the fairies out of paper. The girls had then pinned them to objects to make them look as if they were standing up in the picture. They said they originally thought that the photos would never be shown to anyone but their families and friends. They said they had not wanted to admit it earlier, so that Doyle and others who had believed them would not be subject to embarrassment.

Griffiths, however, insisted all her life that, although they had faked the fairy photos, she really

The title page of Arthur Conan Doyle's 1921 article discussing the evidence for the existence of fairies.

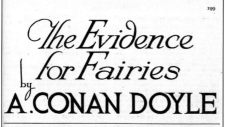

Fairy Stories

"Some of the fairy anecdotes have a curiously convincing air of truth," according to Katharine Briggs, author of *An Encyclopedia of Fairies*, "but at the same time we must make allowance for the constructive power of the imagination in recalling old memories, and for the likelihood that people see what they expect to see."[15]

had seen real fairies in the woods when she was a girl. She said when they made the fairy cutouts they were just trying to reproduce what she had seen.

Much later, in 1997 Paramount Pictures made a movie titled *Fairytale: A True Story* about the girls and their experience.

More Research Is Needed

Some fairy encounters remain mysteries and cannot be totally explained. However, no physical remains, such as the body of a fairy, have ever been found. Until that happens and the remains are examined and identified, most people probably will not believe that fairies really exist. One thing is certain, though. More research is needed into the exciting study of fairy encounters before any real answers will be revealed.

Notes

Chapter 1: The Fairy Kingdom

1. Quoted in Marc Alexander, *British Folklore*. New York: Crescent, 1982, p. 93.
2. Quoted in Janet Bord, *Fairies: Real Encounters with Little People*. New York: Dell, 1997, p. 56.

Chapter 2: Enchanting Encounters

3. Quoted in Alexander, *British Folklore*, p. 106.
4. Quoted in Alexander, *British Folklore*, p. 106.

Chapter 3: Scary Fairies

5. Quoted in Bord, *Fairies*, p. 21.
6. Quoted in Bord, *Fairies*, p. 23.
7. Quoted in Bord, *Fairies*, pp. 31–32.
8. Quoted in Bord, *Fairies*, p. 32.
9. Quoted in Bord, *Fairies*, p. 7.
10. Quoted in Bord, *Fairies*, p. 7.

Chapter 4: Famous Fairy Encounters

11. Quoted in Jerome Clark, *Unexplained! Strange Sightings, Incredible Occurrences & Puzzling Physical Phenomena*. Canton, MI: Visible Ink, 1999, pp. 391–92.
12. Quoted in Clark, *Unexplained!* p. 540.
13. Quoted in Clark, *Unexplained!* p. 541.
14. Quoted in Bord, *Fairies*, p. 131–32.
15. Quoted in Katharine Briggs, *An Encyclopedia of Fairies*. New York: Pantheon, 1976, p. 2.

Glossary

chronicler: A historian who records and reports important events.

enchant: To cast a spell over.

folklorist: A person who studies the stories, beliefs, and customs handed down among the common people of a region or country.

fourth dimension: A place where spirits are believed to live.

heirloom seeds: Seeds that produce plants that are naturally strong and do not require pesticides, herbicides, or fungicides.

hoaxes: Acts that are meant to trick or fool others.

paranormal: Anything that cannot be explained by scientific investigation.

phenomena: Remarkable or unexplained happenings.

second sight: The ability to perceive things beyond the range of ordinary perception.

shape-shifters: Creatures or beings who are able to change to a different shape.

supernatural: Outside or beyond the known laws of nature.

For Further Exploration

Books

Janet Bord, *Fairies: Real Encounters with Little People*. New York: Dell, 1997. This book gives the details about many real-life fairy encounters.

Katharine Briggs, *An Encyclopedia of Fairies*. New York: Pantheon, 1976. In this book Briggs describes all the many types of fairies that are believed to exist.

Jerome Clark, *Unexplained! Strange Sightings, Incredible Occurrences & Puzzling Physical Phenomena*. Canton, MI: Visible Ink, 1999. Clark reports a number of exciting fairy encounters in this book.

Joel Levy, *Guide to the Unexplained*. New York: DK, 2002. General information about fairies as well as many other unanswered mysteries can be found in Levy's book.

Web Sites

The Case of the Cottingley Fairies (www.randi. org/library/cottingley). At this site James Randi reports some of the facts about the Cottingley fairy case. Fairy photos and letters written by Sir Arthur Conan Doyle can be found here.

The Green Children of Woolpit (http://anomaly info.com/articles/sa00022.shtml). Details about the green children case can be found at this site.

Hidden Ireland, a Guide to Irish Fairies (www. irelandseye.com/animation/intro.html). Interesting multimedia Web site, introducing seven different types of Irish fairies and beliefs about them.

Index

Picture Credits

About the Author

Jan Burns writes books, articles, and short stories for both children and adults. She received a bachelor's degree in sociology from the University of California at Berkeley. She lives close to Houston, Texas, with her husband, Don, and sons David and Matt.